LIVING WITH MEANING AND VALUE

Best wishes
David Lamburn

ABOUT THE AUTHOR

The author was born in 1946. He was brought up at Ashdown Farm in the then rural outskirts of Hastings and brought up his own sons, Tim and Chris, for the most part alone, in the Sussex hamlet of Three Oaks. He attended Hastings Grammar School and has a good honours degree in History and Education (Sussex). He had a long career in teaching before retiring as Head of Humanities at Bexhill High School in 1997. He is a former marathon runner and has travelled extensively. He now lives in Boston, Lincolnshire, where the Victorian home he shares with his partner, Sue, overlooks the river and the town's magnificent parish church.

This publication is a development of the ideas first set out by the author in *The Affirmative Way*. His other books are: *How to Pass Exams*; *How to Pass Exams – A Parent's Guide*; *The Lambournes of Ashdown Farm, St. Leonards-on-Sea*; and *Slaney's Act and the Christian Socialists*. He has also contributed to *Political Education and Political Literacy*, edited by Bernard Crick and Alex Porter, and written articles on life at the farm where he was brought up, (*Hastings and St. Leonards Observer* and *Journal of the Wiltshire Family History Society*), on the history of both the Sussex settlements of Hollington and Three Oaks, (*Sussex Family Historian*), and on Boston's Guild of St. Mary, on the connection between Boston's Guildhall and the Pilgrim Fathers and on Thomas Paine, (*Lincolnshire Past and Present*).

LIVING WITH MEANING AND VALUE

David Lambourne

Ash and Oak Books

© Copyright David Lambourne, 2010

ISBN 978-0-9507668-5-0

All Rights Reserved. No part of this publication may be reprinted or reproduced or utilised in any form or by any electronic, mechanical or other means, now known or hereafter invented, including photocopying and recording, or in any information storage or retrieval system, without the prior permission in writing from the publisher.

First published in the United Kingdom in 2010 by
Ash and Oak Books
c/o York Publishing Services, 64 Hallfield Road, Layerthorpe, York, YO31 7ZQ
Email ashandoakbooks@tiscali.co.uk

Prepared, printed and distributed by

York Publishing Services
64 Hallfield Road
Layerthorpe
York
YO31 7ZQ

www.yps-publishing.co.uk

DEDICATION

This essay is dedicated to all those who seek the truth and are open-minded even when cherished ideas are called into question.

CONTENTS

Preface	viii
Introduction	1
A Personal Journey	8
Physical Well-being	15
Living with a Different Perspective	19
Reflection and Meditation	25
Relationships with Others	30
The Teachings of Jesus	39
The Modern World	43
Conclusion	49
Summary	54

PREFACE

I was born and brought up in southern England in an environment in which a rather straightforward and self-contained view of the world seemed to prevail, a view that was greatly influenced by Methodist beliefs and values. Yet, although it was inevitable that my life would in many ways be informed by that simple nonconformist background with its emphasis on frugality, industry, discipline and sobriety, I needed to find my own, more liberal, path. So, my ideas on what is of meaning and value in life came to be formulated many years ago in response to this personal quest for a rational approach to all aspects of living, including the moral and spiritual dimensions, that does not depend on organised religion, that values the life of every human being and that does not place unsustainable demands on planet earth. It was clear then and remains so still that, in this troubled world, money, recognition, status and influence offer no certainties of happiness. I was brought up on a small tenanted farm in an old run down farmhouse without electricity, hot running water, modern sanitation or central heating and in which there was a measure of material impoverishment. The members of my extended family with which I lived had long physically hard working days with little material reward. Yet those close to me were clearly much happier and more contented than many who have so much more appear to be now: many who feel unfulfilled and that life is in some senses unsatisfactory and lacking in worth.

Similarly, it was clear, too, that formal education offers no guarantees either. It seems quite appalling that, even in this age of mass education, so many are driven not by reason but by ignorance, prejudice, superstition and just pure wishful thinking. Formal education is of course to be valued very highly, but I know of those who have had the benefits of a great deal of it who, as well as having considerable intellectual gifts, have been unable to use these advantages to prevent themselves from remaining deeply troubled by life. On the other hand, I know of others who have had only a basic elementary education who are truly happy. Indeed, one friend, who lived in the village where I brought up my sons and who left school at the age of fourteen and never enjoyed any of the apparent advantages of status, wealth or recognition, was, until his death in old age, amongst the wisest, happiest and most contented persons that I have ever met.

I believe that each of us stands to benefit from setting time aside to find out who we really are, how we fit in to the world and how we should live in relation to our fellow human beings. I believe also that, if we are to engage fully in life, we need to curb our extraordinary capacity for selfishness and our inclinations to dwell on the negative, and instead to find our true mission and to develop strategies for that most difficult of tasks: being mindful of and truly experiencing the magic of the present moment.

Such an approach is based on an understanding that much must always remain open to question. We cannot claim to know what we do not know or, as far as can be judged, what is unknowable. This is, in essence, an agnostic position. So, as no definitive answer to the ultimate questions concerning why mankind exists is, certainly at present, possible, we cannot with confidence either affirm or deny the existence of a creative force behind the universe (i.e. a First Cause or creator God).

It is rooted in the conviction that all of us should individually take responsibility for our lives, that all of our fellow humans should be respected irrespective of nationality, class, race, colour, creed, age, gender or sexual orientation and that our intellectual and spiritual resources are capable of enabling us to achieve a knowledge and understanding of both the world and ourselves and to solve many, if not all, of the moral and practical problems which we individually and collectively face.

This approach, however, which emphasises reason rather than faith, does also acknowledge the contribution of the great spiritual teachers, though not necessarily the religious institutions that have developed in their names with their assorted dogmas, rituals and acts of worship. Though such institutions have often served as instruments of social control and as mechanisms for discouraging people to think for themselves, the ideas of the great moral and spiritual teachers, such as Jesus of Nazareth, can in many ways be truly inspirational.

The word spiritual is used throughout this account, not necessarily in a religious sense, but as a means to referring to aspects which are of, pertain to, or emanate from, higher features of the human mind. An agnostic standpoint is consistent with acknowledging the validity of profound spiritual experiences, but requires accepting and explaining them in rational and secular terms rather than necessarily as a result of divine revelation.

This approach acknowledges, too, that in the modern world ignorance, prejudice, bigotry, fundamentalism and despair frequently prevail, whilst those of us who aspire to be rational, liberal and humanitarian and to an environmentally sustainable attitude, too often remain silent.

So, I offer my thoughts in the modest hope that those who realise that there are other measures of success than money, sex and celebrity, who are willing to be a little less self-obsessed, who accept that the present rate of consumption of the world's resources is simply not sustainable, who do recognise a spiritual dimension to their being as well as seek to truly embrace life by connecting in a more positive, satisfying and fulfilling way with their true selves, with others and with the world in general, will find them interesting, helpful and thought-provoking.

David Lambourne

INTRODUCTION

Most of us in the western world today are spared the unremitting toil that made up the lives of the majority of our ancestors just a few generations ago. Lives in which hunger, squalor, disease and the loss of children in infancy or childhood were often experienced. Yet, despite the very many remarkable achievements of mankind, we find the world in which we live is bewildering, complex and dangerous. We find that it is not only a world in which there are continual technological, political, economic and social changes, and one in which traditional beliefs, attitudes and values are constantly being called into question, but one in which the dangers of over-population, global warming, pollution and mass-conflict are threatening to bring human civilisation even to the very edge of the abyss. We find that, in the hectic pace and uncertainty of such a world, it is very easy to overlook our physical and mental well-being, as well as that of others, and drift into a purposeless, and often very stressful, existence based on selfish material or sensual gratification or into a position of resignation to the inevitability of the shortcomings, bewilderment and inadequacies of our predicament, from which the only refuge may be a fantasy life that bears little relation to reality.

To live our lives, however, without considering the worth of what we are doing, so that we largely drift along at the mercy of events and of our own passing whims or moods, is not likely to prove a basis for successful living. Neither, too, will the positive and self-assertive pursuit of pleasure, with its underlying assumption that our happiness will automatically be enhanced by having more of what the world has to offer, be likely to prove any more successful. The unhappy testimonies of many who have achieved 'worldly' success, and who have removed themselves from any clear moral structure so that they feel free to act as they wish, bear witness to the fact that it is possible to have influence, power and status, to travel widely throughout the world and to possess luxurious homes, fine cars and expensive clothes and jewellery, and yet totally lack any sense of meaning in life or any lasting tranquillity of the spirit. In fact, we find that, if we live mainly through selfish desire (i.e. desire that is principally concerned to further our own ends and is deficient in consideration for others) and our desires are frustrated, we are unhappy, if they are partly satisfied, we crave full satisfaction, and even if they are satisfied, we find that they are transferred elsewhere. Indeed, we find that selfish desire, which is not to be confused with the positive need for personal fulfilment, normally breeds on itself so that the satisfaction of one goal leads directly to other, often more inaccessible and unrealistic targets, with the result that happiness and peace in the immediate present is largely undermined by craving, impatience, frustration, anticipation and so on. In looking for alternatives, moreover, we may find that even a life in which we lose ourselves in a blind acceptance of a religious or political ideology, attractive as it may seem, will have its limitations. For we may find ourselves led into absurd and maybe even life-denying behaviour, and will in any case find such a philosophy wanting in our more reflective moments.

The fact is, none of these approaches to existence is likely to result in lasting satisfaction and happiness, for our lives need mature, positive and responsible direction and without it they will be left, for the most part, untouched by qualities such as meaning and wisdom, love and beauty, peace and joy. These are qualities which, as many of various generations, colours, creeds and levels of education have found, are the very essence of a fulfilled and worthwhile life. Fortunately for us these qualities are not unattainable, and it will be argued throughout this short account that, whilst our particular cultures and temperaments will affect the specific routes taken, they can be approached in various rational ways through a conscious and searching response to those two closely related and vitally important questions which ought to be the concern of every human being and to which the brevity of life demands attention sooner rather than later: Who am I? How am I to live?

The importance of the first of these questions has not surprisingly been echoed down through man's history. 'It is', as Pascal has written, 'an extraordinary blindness to live without investigating what we are', for our lives can never prove to be worthwhile without some measure of self-examination. We need to be able to make an honest appraisal of our talents and limitations, to understand and to some extent control our emotional responses and to have some notion of how we fit into the grand scheme of things. In short, we have to learn to establish the right relationship with ourselves, and to establish this relationship we have to have insight into what we ourselves in truth are. In gaining this insight we benefit from the intrinsic value of enquiring into our nature, for the journey is an exciting and fulfilling one in itself, as well as become better able to discriminate and act rationally upon that which is likely to be valuable and meaningful and result in peace, happiness and joy.

Indeed, it is largely because of a lack of self-knowledge that we tend to behave in the often absurd and sometimes insane ways that are so characteristic of human beings. We all have, for instance, an extraordinary and potentially destructive capacity for self-deception. Exaggerated self-display, too, whether in conversation, in dress, in general behaviour or even in our fantasies can cloud our vision and understanding.

We have only to consider how often we have used a conversation for our own ends without really hearing or understanding or being interested in what the other had to say, to realise this. Certainly we all know of others who spend their lives pretending to be what they are not, and whose self-display and self-delusion creates all sorts of problems, pressures and frustrations both for themselves and for those with whom they are associated. We could cite, as an instance, the many people who, though enjoying an adequate standard of material well-being, insist on devoting their entire energies, whether through envy, greed, vanity or self-seeking, to the task of continually increasing their personal wealth often with the object of accumulating more possessions which are of no ultimate worth, and with the result that their whole lives, as well as those of their families, become severely strained, sometimes even to the point of breaking down.

There is, of course, no quick fix to happiness and it may to some extent remain elusive. Many of our personality characteristics are firmly established by adulthood. By beginning to know who we are and how we respond in different situations, however, we can begin to make real and beneficial adjustments to our lives. We can start to act upon that knowledge and to eliminate our inclination towards irrational, unreasonable and absurd behaviour, behaviour which from that point on can only be seen as a profession of ignorance. Of course, the journey to self-knowledge will make us more aware of our own capacity for, and the conflicts arising from, violence, jealousy, wickedness, selfishness, arrogance, pride, greed, fanaticism and so on, but it will bring too the realisation of how destructive these baser aspects of our nature usually are, and how they stand in our way of attaining real peace and wisdom by inhibiting our progress to higher forms of consciousness or awareness.

This new understanding will, in turn, improve our ability to develop the positive or life-affirming aspects, which tend to enhance our ability to live in harmony with ourselves and with others, whilst controlling, even setting aside, the negative or life-denying aspects, of our being. We will thus find that much unnecessary worry, anger, bitterness, fear and the like, can be removed from our lives. But more than this, it will increase our awareness that these are only aspects, as well as enable us to progress more closely to a knowledge of the real essence of our consciousness, of our spirituality. It is when this essence is gradually realised that we really come to fully understand that our fulfilment can never be bound up in the continual development of our egos or in the utmost satisfaction of our mental, emotional and physical cravings, but in the positive flowering of our capacity for wisdom and love and peace and through this of our perception of all the possible beauty and delight of existence.

'As a rule, there is more genuine satisfaction, a truer life, and more obtained from life in the humble cottages of the poor than in the palaces of the rich.'

Andrew Carnegie

A PERSONAL JOURNEY

Today, those of us who choose the path of self-discovery are fortunate in having the cumulative experience and wisdom of many generations to draw on. On an intellectual level, centuries of scientific enquiry, artistic creation and philosophical speculation, though they have produced no coercive proof of a total view of life, have produced, and are producing, an immense amount that is helpful, and in some respects vital, to self-understanding. We can consider, for example, the very significant work which has been, and continues to be done, on the origin and nature of the universe, on the beginning and evolution of life, and on the relationship of both environment and body chemistry to mind and personality. In fact, today, anatomists, philosophers, historians, genealogists, physiologists, anthropologists, biochemists, psychologists, evolutionists, geneticists and others are not only all currently engaged in throwing light on our knowledge of ourselves, but also on directions in which we must pursue this seemingly endless intellectual search further. In this respect we should remember too, that forms of knowledge like art, music, poetry and literature, though they cannot be evidence based in the same way as either science or history, can not only enrich and inspire us but contain truths about the human condition that are equally profound and so help us to learn more about ourselves. To acknowledge each of these points, as we must if we are to successfully embark upon our course, is to automatically elevate the value of learning and education to a position of great importance. Yet though the journey to self-knowledge draws on philosophy, science and religion, on history and genealogy, anthropology and psychology, even on art, literature and music, it is a personal spiritual, and not just an intellectual, journey. Intellect will, by itself, take us only so far.

This can be illustrated by considering our relationship to the emergence of our own culture and environment. We may come, for instance, to 'know', in the limited sense of the word, how we (i.e. mankind) have evolved through stages from the simplest forms of life, how the natural resources on which we have come to depend were formed, how and when the tools and machinery that we use were invented and improved, and how our ancestors lived out their lives in circumstances very different from our own, without ever gaining any real insight into, or sense of closeness with, our historical and anthropological roots. The point that we are what we are because of the evolution of our planet and the lives of our ancestors on it needs to be grasped by the spirit and not just the mind, needs to be approached through intuition and insight as well as the intellect, needs to be felt as something real and not just known to be true. In the same way we not only need to 'know' about our dependence on other people and on the forces of nature in the present time, but 'feel' also a sense of harmony with the world in which we live.

The spiritual dimension is needed because, in its central aspects, knowing what it is to be a man or woman involves us in looking searchingly into what it is to be the particular men or women we alone are, and in confronting the mysteries and delights of our own awareness. It involves us in examining our unique centres of consciousness, from which, too, we can observe our circumstances and opportunities, our abilities, potential and shortcomings, our bodies, thoughts and emotions, and even those of our decisions which might affect what we will become in the future. It can eventually involve us as well, through persistence, honesty and determination, in pressing on beyond our senses, attitudes, thoughts and emotions to attain, through losing ourselves in contemplation, the highest levels of consciousness or awareness in which are completeness, wholeness and integration and in which we experience, however dimly, the universe as the unity its name implies. (This is the profound experience which many would describe as finding God, but that others identify with, without ascribing to it revelation from a divine being, as a defining moment of self-realisation). It is here in particular that intellectual understanding will itself prove insufficient and we will need to experience truth as a reality, for to penetrate to a deep insight into our existence is essentially a personal spiritual experience. In other words, we must ourselves personally embark upon the quest for self-knowledge. This certainly does not mean that we should in any way set reason aside, but it does mean that we cannot achieve success solely by drawing on the recorded accounts and recommendations of others.

Of course, the suggestion that the quest for self-discovery will lead us to consider the way to what has variously been described as integration, liberation, salvation, wholeness, enlightenment and so on, may initially seem objectionable on the grounds that it smacks of religious speculation. It is true that most religious systems consist of much which is irrational and indeed positively unhelpful to those who desire true self-knowledge, partly because many of the ideas of moral and spiritual leaders have become enshrined in dogma, which is always questionable and frequently divisive, and become distorted by the power and rituals of the institutions which have grown around them and the blind faith that these have so often encouraged. Yet many religious and mystical writers have, in differing ways, through the limitations of their languages, cultures and religious traditions, confirmed that we can, through, and in the process of, stilling our minds and receptively pondering, aspire, albeit perhaps only dimly, to the great liberating or enlightening experience of penetrating to the centre, to the ground of our being, which exists if only as a necessary abstraction, beyond our selfish cravings, desires and fantasies, to the point of seeing ourselves and Reality, whatever we may conceive it to be, as we and it really are, and to the point of an awareness of a sense of oneness. In short, they show us that there is a peace to be found amidst the trials and tribulations of life and that it is not determined by or bound up with some neat theological formula.

Such a goal can only be progressively and never totally or permanently attained. Levels of insight will deepen, but there will always remain the capacity for further enrichment. Nevertheless, it is a vital experience to know we are in Reality, to realise that we are a manifestation of Reality itself, and it is an experience which has the power to transform our lives, particularly in so far as it helps us to act with impartiality and harmony rather than with individuality and selfishness, and to see things in the most sympathetic, favourable, constructive and understanding way.

The fact that we ourselves must personally embark upon the quest for self-knowledge does, however, mean that the task is by no means an easy one. Certainly, self-control, determination, honesty, self-discipline and a positive outlook are all needed in considerable portions, as indeed they are if any worthwhile goal in life is to be achieved. Equally important are humility and a child-like sense of wonder, for without these we will lack clearness and simplicity of vision. The intellectual and spiritual journey requires, too, that we acknowledge that there are many questions to which we do not know the answers. It requires that we accept that we are products of our environment, our cultural, religious, racial and family backgrounds and that we are, along with all others, prone to failures and weaknesses. It requires that we identify our particular frailties and failures, which itself demands that we also accept and even forgive the frailties and failures of others, and that we strip away the outer layers of pretence and so cause many of our cherished ideas about ourselves in particular, and mankind in general, to prove illusory. It is only by becoming truly aware of how we think and feel in different situations and with others that we can make positive adjustments to our inner lives. Such empowerment will, for example, enable us to identify the sources of our fears and so come to terms with them. It will enable us to use every experience, however adverse, to make ourselves stronger and more confident. It will also enable us to recognise that sadness is not a negative emotion but one which needs to be experienced and is central to how we grow as people. We may not always like what we find, we may discover paradoxes within ourselves and we will almost certainly have to revisit painful experiences, yet we will find that these results can be handled with honesty and humility when put in the perspective of our progressive awareness of the great unifying experience of oneness and we will be empowered by a sense of both balance and confidence in life.

If we are to be successful we have especially to learn the great value of self-control in all aspects of life, for mastery over simple everyday things is essential before mastery over important matters can be established. We have to learn, too, to live undemandingly and not always see ourselves, as the selfish and self-assertive do, as the centre of all being. In truth, the task has to be of vital importance to us, mattering more than such as the pursuit of wealth, celebrity, sexuality or position. Yet though the task is difficult, it is not unattainable. If attainment were limited to a select priesthood pursuing it as a full-time occupation it would be of little use to the ordinary man or woman. In fact, we can all be successful if we are prepared to recognise the great possibilities which exist within ourselves.

'There is no need to run outside
For better seeing,
Nor to peer from a window. Rather abide
At the centre of your being;
For the more you leave it, the less you learn.'

Lao-Tze

PHYSICAL WELL-BEING

It might be appropriate to consider at this stage that these possibilities are more likely to reach fruition if we develop and maintain, so far as we are able, a high level of physical well-being. Physical health makes us feel buoyant and youthful, tends to make our minds more tranquil and temperaments more placid, and gives us a greater zest for living. It enables us to have a more heightened sense of awareness, improved concentration and an increased capacity to work efficiently and for long stretches without fatigue. Indeed, physical health is a highly desirable factor in all aspects of our journey. Not only can physical activity in itself enhance self-knowledge, but if we are in good health we are more likely to be able to sustain the interest and energy needed for intellectual enquiry, to be able to calm our minds for reflection and meditation and to be able to more vigorously serve our fellows. There are many different approaches to the establishment and maintenance of physical health, but broadly the areas on which we should concentrate are as follows.

We should maintain an adequate, well-balanced, natural diet, and prevent ourselves from becoming overweight. We should ensure that we breathe correctly, that is in a relaxed and controlled manner, (this will help us to calm and control our minds), and that we allow ourselves sufficient time for relaxation and sleep. We should ensure that we do not weaken or even destroy our bodies through tobacco or harmful drugs (legal or otherwise), and this we can do by abstaining from them. We should ensure that our consumption of alcohol is, at the most, moderate, though even this is hardly to be recommended. Apart from anything else it is not only self-indulgent and self-destructive to drink to excess, but is contrary to the objective of self-realisation which is the fulfilment and not the distortion or repression of consciousness. Finally, we should ensure that, so far as our basic age and health permits, we take regular and sustained exercise, such as running, walking or swimming, or through active sports or a scientifically designed fitness programme.

Not only is physical well-being likely to prove of value to us in following this way of approaching life, but conversely, we will find too that the pursuit of this path will itself have a beneficial effect on our health. It has already been suggested that if we are to aspire to certain aspects of self-realisation we have to become masters over our own minds. If we accomplish this, and in turn our improving health will increase the degree to which we can do so, we will have, amongst other things, brought our emotions under control, not by suppression but by being realistic, and this is something which is vital for lasting and harmonious health. It is now recognised by medical science that emotional stresses and what are usually dark negative emotions like insecurity, guilt, worry, fear, frustration, jealousy, anger and hatred are responsible for, or a contributory factor to, a wide range of complaints such as coronary thrombosis and high blood pressure, and generally poison the body and destroy peace of mind. On the other hand, the bright positive emotions like love, joy and hope, tend to protect us from harmful stress, have a beneficial influence on bodily health and generally lead us to a richer and fuller life. It is only when we have learnt to still the mind's turbulence, to confront our feelings rationally, and to develop a considerable measure of detachment that we will be free from the tyranny of the destructive dark emotions and be able to concentrate on those which are positive and bright. Self-mastery, then, is not only a necessary part of self-realisation, but is also an important contributory factor in the establishment and maintenance of physical health.

'Go out in the world and do well – but, more importantly, go out in the world and do good.'

Anon

LIVING WITH A DIFFERENT PERSPECTIVE

In general, there can be little doubt that the more we progress on our quest the better potentially our health becomes. But this is only one direction in which our lives stand to be transformed, for when we begin to earnestly ask the basic questions about the meaning of life we embark upon a course which is bound to be of great consequence: a course which requires us to aspire to new levels of consciousness in relation to ourselves, others and the world in which we live. We become increasingly aware that taken from a separate or an isolated point of view, our personal nature is, in the context of the almost incomprehensible duration and magnitude of our universe, both insignificant and transitory, and that to live in a purely selfish manner is utterly pointless. Indeed, any notion that we might have that a wholly independent existence is possible comes to seem not only erroneous but also absurd in the light of the knowledge of how dependent we are on the forces of nature and how fleeting and microscopically small one life is in the context of the great cosmological extents of time and space. On the contrary, all aspects of our lives seem not independent but interdependent with others and with our environment, whether it be socially, emotionally, linguistically, intellectually, physically or whatever. Our egoism may still kick at and strive against this, but we come to see that it is something from which we cannot escape.

We become increasingly aware, too, that, contrary to the popular notion that success is found through wealth and ambition, striving in the pursuit of external rewards for their own sake, such as with social status or recognition, or a level of material prosperity above that needed for the practical purpose of providing reasonably for the basic requirements of life, (it will be noted that this is very different from the misguided idea of making a virtue of poverty), is empty, futile and vain, a likely source of much unhappiness and a barrier to the establishment of real joy in our lives. We become aware, also, that the harbouring of anger, resentment, bitterness or prejudice towards others is pointless and potentially destructive and that the hope, expectation or even gratification of a wide variation of sexual desire is equally futile and unlikely to yield lasting joy or even satisfaction. In other words, because as we progress in self-knowledge we come to realise that what we are is of more value than what we have and that our basic problems are in some considerable measure caused by our constant want, crave or desire and by our stubbornness and pride, we come to gradually change our attitudes and life-style accordingly.

Of course, it could be argued that to seek self-knowledge is itself to selfishly want or desire something, and is therefore equally unsatisfactory. The point here, though, is that what is being pursued is what is ultimately true, worthwhile and satisfying. But not only this, we find that the path to self-knowledge is itself meaningful and of value. It is at least as much about travelling with a different point of view as with arriving at a destination and, because of this, our lives become concentrated much more on the present moment than on allowing life to pass us by by looking constantly forward to the next source of satisfaction, or on dwelling on what happened in the past. We learn to overcome our inclination to eagerly anticipate future moments which are themselves never really experienced because they only serve as times for further planning. (Although it would clearly be totally wrong to infer from this that hope and planning for, and commitment, especially through well-defined objectives, to, the future are unnecessary or that we should act with scant regard for the consequences of our behaviour). We come, too, to realise that constant striving prevents us from making the best of the present. Hitherto, for instance, we may have dreamt about what we could do if and when we rose to positions of influence yet have completely overlooked the immediate opportunities. We may never have appreciated that the man or woman in a 'lowly' position may very well be able to offer as least as much practical service to his or her fellows as one that holds some 'high' office. We may never have appreciated either, that we could so easily fall into the trap of so many who have striven for one objective after another until their lives have faded, probably prematurely, and have been left with never having experienced a sense of what is worthwhile or of knowing who they were.

The fact is, that with systematic attention, we may come to a state of 'mindfulness', to draw the most from, and so rejoice in, the here and now, and realise that it is only here that there is Reality and only now that we can see, feel and, above all, be; that in Time everything is becoming and therefore incomplete, but in the present moment there is encapsulated completeness and wholeness. We become more inclined to value every moment as precious and to accept life as the gift it is so that our selfish aspirations and expectations can gradually be replaced by spiritual peace and tranquillity. Amongst other things, our concern to live in the present affects our attitude to the daily round and the common task. In recognising the value of living one moment at a time, even the most mundane of occupations comes, for example, to be done properly, with pleasure and for its own sake and not only its rewards or results.

Our lives, then, stand to be changed in important respects. As we progress in self-knowledge the burden of the need for wealth, position, power or status becomes stripped away, and we come to find joy through disinterestedness in personal outward success. We come to look on and accept all experiences as opportunities to learn about ourselves. In this way we can accept, even welcome, difficult situations as means to deepen our own characters and self-awareness. With this attitude, even the ultimate and inevitable experience of death with its likely finality can be approached with both dignity and a sense of adventure and can, in the meantime, enable us to value each moment as precious. We come, too, to no longer suffer any unnecessary level of harmful stress (perhaps better labelled as distress) which the world had formerly thrust upon us because we come to have the knowledge and inclination necessary to avoid or cope with many of the situations that create it. We come to develop, as is essential for happiness, a realistic understanding and acceptance of the restrictions our circumstances in life impose upon us and of our own individual practical talents, capacity and potential, and to see the utter futility of getting anxious over that which is beyond our abilities to influence. Similarly, even if we might be genetically predisposed to bouts of depression, by learning about ourselves we can come to recognise the factors that trigger it and to adopt coping strategies to minimise its impact. In fact, we come to learn to 'let go' of our egotistical desires and inclinations, to put our problems and difficulties in perspective by pondering on our true nature, and to live, through spiritual insight, the simple, uncomplicated and harmonious life that makes possible, and at the same time arises out of, both a lasting inner serenity and stillness, and a loving and co-operative attitude towards our fellow human beings.

'It is not about having what we want but wanting what we have.'

Dalai Lama

REFLECTION AND MEDITATION

There can be little doubt that in progressing towards these objectives, though ultimately we must discover our own way, we can find the examples of the great moral and spiritual teachers valuable. Certainly even institutional religion can, providing it is liberal, undogmatic, critical and empirical, offer endless opportunities for self-discovery and experiment. All the higher religions contain important spiritual truths, even though they tend to 'dress them up' in poetic and mythical language or in ritual. (Thus the Biblical personalisation of evil as Satan or the Devil, and of truth, and love and reality as God). There are, of course, considerable differences between, and even within, various religious systems, although similar truths are often stated in very different ways, but this only serves to indicate the many varied paths to self-realisation. In fact, spiritual teachers of greatly differing persuasions can, along with philosophers independent of any orthodox religion, provide us with a wide range of intellectual and spiritual ideas upon which we can profitably reflect.

Obviously, too, and more specifically, religion is likely to be particularly helpful, if we are to aspire to that knowledge which is found only on the highest dimensions of consciousness, in the guidance it can offer on the value and techniques of meditation. Most of the great moral and spiritual teachers indicate clearly, in their various ways, that by stilling the mind and looking steadily within, we can grow, even amidst life's constant toil, in peace, joy and compassion and in what can be described as eternal life. They show that by focussing our minds on, for example, a single object, idea or sound and by gently bringing our minds back to it when they stray we can reach a state of genuine mental relaxation. They show that by regular and disciplined meditation and contemplation we can, in our quest for self-awareness, be progressively liberated from anxiety, guilt and selfish desire, from envy, self-assertion and excessive personal ambition, and from all other motives which conflict with the welfare of others and with the worthwhile values in human life.

In order to become masters of meditation we have to develop certain powers. Thus, we have to improve our powers of concentration, to learn to withdraw ourselves from the distractions of the outside world, to become capable of observing ourselves in a detached way, to establish control, albeit through gentleness and patience, over our thoughts, emotions and desires, and to adopt both a positive and understanding attitude to life. In short, we have to develop the capacity for the degree of awareness of our own awareness that we will need if we are to penetrate towards the centre of the meaning of our existence.

Having developed these powers, our controlled minds can more successfully reflect on and contemplate the great intellectual and spiritual truths, especially as set down in the writings of spiritual teachers and philosophers, and find, in the stillness of meditation, insight and inspiration. (True insights and inspirations, it must be said, never contradict reason but are based on and fulfil it). No longer need we be prevented from observing our true selves by our selfish cravings and desires, by our anxieties, resentments and moods and by the turbulence of our thoughts, but become able to begin, despite our spiritual imperfections, to penetrate towards the highest levels of realisation. It is on these that, in a moment of surrender, we may come to feel, perhaps only dimly and very briefly, that awareness of an encounter with something which, amid the great unfathomable mysteries of life, is unambiguous, and, though it cannot be captured in some neat theological formula and is itself unexplainable, in a sense calls for no further explanation. This is the experience referred to earlier which may happen wherever we are at peace, such as in a simple sanctuary chapel of a medieval church or on a quiet cliff top overlooking the sea. It is the experience which has variously been described as integration, salvation, enlightenment, the peace of God which passes all understanding and so on. The state of total union with Reality, whatever we conceive it to be, and whether we deify it or not, (and for many this real experience may ultimately seem explainable in secular as opposed to religious terms), in which is found the deep spiritual experience of the unity or oneness of life.

This sense of oneness, which incidentally finds support in many areas of science especially, perhaps, ecology, brings with it the feeling that everything is connected to everything else, from the mightiest of the stars to a tiny grain of sand, from the minutest single living cell to the most complex human organism, all ultimately related and deserving of reverence and respect. In losing ourselves in this experience we are able to experience a rapid outgoing of fear, desire, worry, frustration and egoism and to find instead an inner peace, relaxation and joy in which we are released from the burdens of self. As, moreover, we are progressively calmed by the stillness at the centre of our being we become not only more aware of what we really are and of our rootedness in life, but also find a new dynamic and vital power to live and a deeper consciousness of our relatedness to others.

'Do not dwell in the past, do not dream of the future, concentrate the mind on the present moment.'

Buddha

RELATIONSHIPS WITH OTHERS

This observation brings us more directly to the second question outlined at the beginning of this essay: How am I to live? For although it is desirable that we pursue the intellectual and spiritual way to self-knowledge and live the kind of simple and uncomplicated life that makes this possible, this journey is no escapist one, and will cause us not only to comprehend the 'idea', and experience the 'feeling', of unity with our fellow men and women, but also to take account of the fact that, in 'practice', we cannot live in isolation but must live in a real world in association with others. The need for self-knowledge includes the need for practical knowledge of, and concern for, our relationship both to the world in which we live and to those with whom we share the world. As a consequence, self-knowledge makes greater love for, and harmony with, the world and others possible, whilst at the same time is itself advanced by love and harmony, and the extent to which we successfully take account of this, will regulate, to a considerable degree, the quality of our lives. In short, we come to realise that how we live has to be informed above all else by how we see and treat others.

It is true that it seems somewhat paradoxical to suggest that having experienced a sense of oneness or unity with others we should then have to acknowledge them as distinct centres of consciousness. Yet logic dictates that this is precisely the case if we are not to deny both the worth and the existence of every single aspect of our own individuality. Having acknowledged this we have to recognise that reason also dictates that we have a duty to treat others as we would have them treat us, unless, in particular circumstances, there are relevant reasons for not doing so, and that we cannot expect others to perform their duties to themselves, their families and the wider community if we are not prepared to perform ours. We have to recognise, moreover, that the extent to which the unique aspects of our being can have status depends, as well as on self-respect, on concern and respect for uniqueness in other persons, whatever their race, colour, creed, gender, age or sexual orientation and irrespective of whether we happen to like them or not, and on the sharing of our personal lives in communion or fellowship with them. This is a central principle which cannot ever be compromised by any particular concepts of justice or toleration that may be in vogue at any one time.

In this regard, we have to recognise the value and motivating power of love, which is a psychological need which we all have. So, if we accept, as seems logical, that all intentional acts or statements which unnecessarily directly or indirectly harm or hurt another human being are immoral, then we can see that love, which, incidentally, is not sentimental but includes amongst its ingredients courage, tenacity and strength, and respect for persons are the guiding principles whereby we can enter the moral life. For not only do they offer guidance for the close relationships which we enter into personally, such as and especially within our families, (a happy, permanent family is after all a great stabilising influence among the uncertainties of the modern world), but will lead us to treat all people as ends in themselves and never as means to our own ends. (Lying, stealing, insulting or abusive behaviour and sexual exploitation will be seen by us to be wrong, for instance, because they involve treating others as means and not ends and are devoid of respect for them). They can even guide our attitudes on national and international problems, such as economic conflict, war and poverty, through an acknowledgement that all human beings are worthy of respect just because they are human beings. (Although, in an evil world, this does not necessarily always rule out conflict, since those political systems which genuinely attempt to uphold social justice, individual freedom, rights and responsibility, and respect for persons, are, in this respect, worth defending. But even here it has to be remembered that non-violent, passive resistance has an extraordinary potential).

It has already been hinted at, too, that it is impossible to comprehend any such rational approach to moral life being successful without a measure of self-knowledge. For we find that issues are not always clear on a morality so conceived, and unless we are clear about ourselves and our own motives, the criteria we accept are likely to be largely our own inventions in the sense that they are more likely to fit features of our own minds about which we are ignorant than to fit the facts of the real world. Similarly, this approach to life demands that we develop the ability to communicate with our fellows. For, on the one hand, since no psychological or philosophical textbook can ever tell us all the facts we need to know about every particular case, it is essential to develop our own perceptivity and awareness of other people so that we may know their needs. Whilst, on the other hand, we need the communication with, and understanding of, our fellow men and women in order that we ourselves may be helped to be rational. Without the constant intercourse of thought and feeling we would find it no easy matter to maintain an awareness of ourselves and our difficulties and challenges.

Indeed, the knowledge and ability to communicate, if accompanied with the insight of a sense of oneness, can provide the basis of real understanding between ourselves and others; a level on which we can all stand on an equal footing. In this sense we will be able to see ourselves in the behaviour or spiritual life of others, and with this insight, the human passions, love, hate and so on, become the problems of not only others but ourselves also. We will see, too, that, despite our apparent differences and despite the outward personas we adopt, we are all fundamentally on the same journey, we are all trying to make our way in life but are all frail and flawed and, in varying proportions, we are all touched by the range of human experiences. Wealth or position cannot prevent sorrow or poverty the experience of joy. Thus we will see that whatever is existent in us can be found in others and vice versa, and that, despite injustices and inequalities, others experience joy and sorrow, pleasure and pain, others live in the same world and others share in many ways the same aspirations. By coming to have this perspective, so that we come to recognise all humans as brothers and sisters (a position that is supported by modern genetics which demonstrates that the differences between individuals are small compared with the similarities), there can be true harmony, true peace, true understanding between us and our fellows. By coming to have this perspective, too, we will recognise that no human beings are wholly good or wholly bad so that none of us are fit to stand in judgement of others. A view that will even lead us to recognise that we should have concern, understanding and compassion not only for the victims of evil but for the perpetrators as well.

If we attempt to approach life in this way, with the tolerance and acceptance of others and impartiality and equanimity that such an approach demands, we will find that we will not be very successful if, in the process, we also attempt to use each situation to specifically derive some personal pleasure from it or to exaggerate our own egos. On the contrary, we will achieve the greatest success only if we think, speak or act because we know or feel that it is the right and rational thing to do. Often this will involve loving impartially and selflessly as though just for the sake of loving. Nevertheless, even though we cannot be very successful if we directly and consciously seek personal benefits, it is certain that personal spiritual benefits will come. Experience will show that by adopting an attitude of love, respect and consideration for others we will ourselves be greatly enriched. For, although we will not seek it, in exercising our moral duty and in co-operating with others, we will increase our own satisfaction by experiencing a sense of inner well-being. In addition, by exercising various spiritual qualities in loving and serving others we will grow in those qualities. Thus we will grow kinder by being kind, more gentle by being gentle, more understanding, compassionate and tolerant by being understanding, compassionate and tolerant. We will find that our own well-being will be enhanced by our willingness to forgive the shortcomings of others and that love, too, tends to call out its own response, so that if we love we are more likely to be loved and find the barriers of fear and distrust broken down.

By adopting this approach, moreover, we can add a deep sense of meaning and purpose to our lives. For it is through adopting this approach that we will be led to realise that success and significance in our lives consists, to a large degree, in co-operation with others and in the contributions we can make to their lives. We will see that, whilst the rational basis for respecting others does imply that we should also respect and seek to fulfil ourselves, we cannot give anything but a private meaning to our lives if we lack 'fellow feeling' and social interest.

It would be absurd to imagine that it could be otherwise. Our weaknesses and limitations make it impossible to realise our aims in isolation. If we lived entirely alone and tried to meet our problems by ourselves we would perish. (This is even truer in the modern world than ever before. As just one instance, almost every article that we purchase links us either directly or indirectly to hundreds, perhaps thousands, of people who have been involved in its design, production, distribution, sale and so on). In fact, since consciousness is itself at least partly a social product, a solitary life lived from birth and which had been lived without access to a verbal or linguistic community would be lived through, what in ordinary human terms, would amount to little more than unconscious behaviour.

Clearly, without others, we would be unable to continue either our own lives or the life of mankind. We are always tied to other men and women. This is why there is a great need for love and why association is the greatest step for the welfare of each individual, for that of each community, as well as for that of mankind itself. We need to come to recognise this and to know that we can come to find challenge and fulfilment in the service of others. We need to recognise, too, our affinity with all those in the human process – those that have lived before, those that are living now and those that are as yet unborn – and know that this is the time in which we can fulfil our creative tasks, and, by having the relevant knowledge and by being understanding, tolerant, disciplined and positive in both thought and action, make our contribution to mankind.

If we fail to recognise these points or refuse to act for the good of others we will not only have missed out on the joy that can be experienced through being involved in causes greater than ourselves, but have betrayed our connection with the human race, denied the contributions of the past and, as a consequence, relinquished all claim on the future. In short, we will come to know that, whilst others may be more gifted and capable, whilst our own abilities, talents, opportunities and circumstances will impose limitations on us, and whilst our efforts may go largely unrecognised or we find that in standing firm on the principles of respect and service many opportunities for worldly achievement may pass us by, we are nevertheless guilty of a sin of omission if we withhold what we have to give, and that we can only find a lasting meaning and purpose by proving ourselves good 'fellow men', that is, by living, without directly seeking reward, the kind of life of service envisaged by Horace Mann who instructed: 'Be ashamed to die until you have won some victory for humanity'.

'Whatever is my right as a man is the right of another; and it becomes my duty to guarantee as well as to possess.'

Thomas Paine

THE TEACHINGS OF JESUS

Such ideas are much informed by that great moral and spiritual teacher Jesus of Nazareth, who went to great lengths to point out the duty of each person to love and serve others, particularly those in need; the hungry, the naked, the homeless, the sick, the captive and the stranger, together with the drug addict, the drunkard, the prostitute, the criminal and all those who are physically, mentally and emotionally damaged, and to be forgiving and non-judgemental of our fellows. They reflect those of Jesus, too, in so far as they propose that we as individuals should be concerned not primarily with theologies and creeds but with people, and should recognise the eternal, transforming power of love. Love, which can overcome fear and distrust, which can be effective even when extended to enemies, and which can win victories over envy, hatred and falsehood. They are consistent with the teachings of Jesus to the extent that he stressed that we must humbly acknowledge our limitations and weaknesses, lose our love of worldly things, give up our personal selfish lives and follow his example in devoting our time, knowledge and energy, through love and service, to the welfare of others, if we are to discover what he described as 'the life everlasting'; the abundant life. Whatever sophisticated arguments traditional theologians might construct, the essence of Jesus's teachings, which can largely be interpreted in a secular manner, is love and living a good and fulfilled life.

Of course, the suggestion that the whole approach embodied in this essay, both to the need for self-knowledge and to that of love and respect for others, is entirely consistent with an undogmatic and liberal interpretation of Christianity, may cause a somewhat unsympathetic reaction amongst traditionalist Christians. But if we accept without question the proposition that the Bible is the literal word of God or that Jesus was literally the son of God then we are like the person who would build his house on quicksand. If we simply accept the doctrines or dogmas of a religious institution, one of the primary functions of which is as an instrument of social control, then we are abdicating our responsibility to think for ourselves. If, on the other hand, we read the Bible in general and the teachings of Jesus in particular with an open mind, we may well learn a great deal about the human condition, about ourselves, and about how to live our lives in a harmonious and meaningful way. It has always to be remembered that Jesus taught in the context of his own religious and cultural tradition and as such used language that was very often poetic rather than literal. (When he said, for example, that 'he that eateth my flesh, and drinketh my blood, dwelleth in me', he was not talking in literal terms). If we acknowledge this, we can come to understand the great spiritual truths to which Jesus referred, particularly his claim that sin (perhaps, in many ways, better described as ignorance) is enslaving, and his promise that 'ye shall know the truth and the truth shall make you free'. In short, if we recognise the role of myths and mythology in connection with religious understanding we can develop a concept of Jesus as an inspirational teacher, who suggested how we might best live our lives, that is not necessarily dependent on his being part of a divine force.

We may even conclude, that, especially for those of us with a Christian heritage, the way to life has never been signposted more clearly than by Jesus and that the Christian concept of all humans as brothers and sisters, which renders it unnecessary to draw distinctions between people on any arbitrary basis and which finds confirmation in the spiritual experience of a sense of oneness, is a very appealing one. Certainly not only can the experience and contribution of Jesus serve as an inspiration, but, if we sincerely seek the truth and not only believe in such as love, beauty and goodness but accept the need to assume the possibility of these qualities in perfection, we may come to have, at the least in a poetic and abstract sense, an idea of the Christian God. (Thus: 'everyone that loveth is born of God and knoweth God'.)

'Love thy neighbour as thyself.'

Jesus of Nazareth

THE MODERN WORLD

The foregoing is, then, the essence of a process that arises out of those two questions: Who am I? How am I to live? and, as such, involves pursuing self-knowledge and awareness and living with all men and women in a spirit of love, respect, co-operation and service. It is a way which is based on rational, liberal and humanitarian values that are unfettered by dogma and which, besides being capable of benefiting us personally, is in complete harmony with the global challenges of the modern world; a world which so many (such as Einstein who argued that 'the world must be one or it will be none') feel to be on a threshold, and one in which there is a lack, not of knowledge and skills (or at least of their potential) necessary to solve its problems, but merely of sufficient goodwill. The problems of the world are not generally caused or exacerbated by being addressed in an intellectual or reasoned manner, but by ignorance, neglect or negative and often long-standing emotional responses such as with many of the disputes between religious, national or cultural groups. The idea that people matter simply because they are people is, then, the principle most likely to heal the divisions between peoples of differing political or religious creeds and to induce co-operation on the major problems confronting mankind.

In fact, the combination into one way of the simple spiritual and intellectual life, which carries with it a low level of material need, with the desire to extend love and respect to all men and women, if accepted on a large scale, would make possible a fair and responsible stewardship of the earth's resources, which we certainly cannot carry on using up at the present unsustainable rate. It would also make possible co-operation in redistributing the world's wealth so as to raise the standard of living in the Third World, a serious attempt to resolve the population crisis and a reduction in the self-assertion and aggressive greed which inevitably breeds aggression and hostility. It has, moreover, the capacity to prevent further holocausts or incidents of apartheid or ethnic cleansing and could even lead to the nations of the world laying down their arms and channelling the enormous resources which they had hitherto spent on war and preparation for war into constructing a new environmentally friendly, co-operative, non-violent world order. The latter is perhaps the greatest challenge before mankind and the greatest cause to which human beings could commit themselves at this point in history.

Many cynics and pessimists argue that, as basic human nature remains largely unaltered, such hopes are unrealistic and that the lessons of history confirm this. We are reminded daily through news bulletins of how thin and fragile the veneer of civilisation is. Yet if individuals and communities retreat from rationality and abandon standards of decency the logic of the arguments set out here are as powerful and compelling as ever. People are no less in need of love and respect in societies where barbarism exercises its grip nor are communities any less in need of those willing to act for the common good.

The more optimistic will prefer to find encouragement in the profound cultural changes that have happened. For example, in western culture attitudes to both slavery and child labour have been transformed during the past two hundred years. Certainly, though, raising everyone's awareness to the seemingly novel, though obviously logical, idea of treating everyone else as we ourselves would be treated is not going to be an easy task. Those who are currently unwilling or unable to be open-minded and brave enough to take this journey will require sensitive guidance from those that are. Fortunately, however, there are already many within each of the nations of the world who recognise the way forward and accept that if mankind is to progress, even survive, our species has little alternative to adopting an outlook which is capable of addressing the issues of mass destruction, terrorism, global warming, unsustainable demands on the world's finite resources and other problems which we collectively face. The following extract from the Belgrade Charter, which was drawn up more than a generation ago, is quoted at length to underline the point:

> The recent United Nations Declaration for a New International Economic Order calls for a new concept of development – one which takes into account the satisfaction of the needs and wants

of every citizen of the earth, of the pluralism of societies and of the balance and harmony between humanity and the environment. What is being called for is the eradication of the basic causes of poverty, hunger, illiteracy, pollution, exploitation and domination......

It is absolutely vital that the world's citizens insist upon measures that will support the kind of economic growth which will not have harmful repercussions on people; that will not in any way diminish their environment and their living conditions. It is necessary to find ways to ensure that no nation should grow or develop at the expense of another nation and that the consumption of no individual should be increased at the expense of other individuals. The resources of the world should be developed in ways which will benefit all of humanity and provide the potential for raising the quality of life for everyone.

We need nothing short of a new global ethic – an ethic which espouses attitudes and behaviour for individuals and societies which are consonant with humanity's place within the biosphere; which recognises and sensitively responds to the complex and ever-changing relationships between humanity and nature and between people. Significant changes must occur in all of the world's nations to assure the kind of rational development which will be guided by this new global ideal – changes which will be directed towards an equitable distribution of the world's resources and more fairly satisfy the needs of all peoples...... Above all, it will demand the assurance of perpetual peace through co-existence and co-operation among nations with different social systems.

Clearly, the concepts set out in this essay, which cut across the ever-changing pattern of race, culture and creed, could provide the basis for this new global ethic and the necessary psychological adjustment to it, for if enough men and women were prepared to seek harmony (oneness) and understanding, to overcome many of their own personal selfish desires and work instead for the benefit of the wider community, and to act with love, humility, compassion and a sense of responsibility, genuine care for the environment, true world peace and the eradication of the obscenities of poverty, injustice, ignorance, inequality and so on would surely become possible. Of course, there are those who argue that this is a forlorn hope. Yet many have reached a position where they are truly capable of living in harmony with others, irrespective of background, culture, religion or nationality, and in a manner which does not make excessive demands on the environment and if they have, many others can too. In short, these values are capable of ushering in a new age of morality for mankind, in which men and women would not, whether through wealth, power, position or status, seek to dominate their fellow human beings.

'Every day is a fresh beginning,
Listen my soul to the glad refrain.
And, spite of old sorrows
And older sinning,
Troubles forecasted
And possible pain,
Take heart with the day and begin again.'

Susan Coolidge

CONCLUSION

As for us as individuals, the implications for our own lives of such an approach are immediate and far-reaching. We must constantly guard against drifting into a life of what is best described as quiet desperation or of being unwittingly seduced by the security of some prevailing ideology or by the illusion that through constantly striving to advance our economic and social standing in society we can automatically bring increased benefit to ourselves or to others. (Although, of course, it has to be acknowledged than in fulfilling our creative tasks or in seeking to serve others we may achieve something to which others attach importance or significance or be drawn by circumstances to a position of prosperity or influence, in which case we have a responsibility to ensure that, in humility, the creative impulse or the spirit of service remains of primary importance.) The fact is that the abundant life is not something we will find only after we have accumulated a given number of material possessions of a specific quality or fulfilled certain personal ambitions for status (for selfish desire is, as has been shown, largely misplaced desire), or only after some undefined date in the future when our society has been reconstructed. Instead, this approach can, providing it is of overwhelming importance to us, mattering more than wealth, sensual pleasure, power, status or occupation, put us on the path towards spiritual and moral goodness and so offer us the possibility of a meaningful, worthwhile and serene life in the here and now.

The fact that it requires this kind of commitment does not, however, mean that it is a merely speculative philosophy, for its pursuit has implications for every aspect of our practical lives. It comes to affect our attitude to family life, where we have to recognise the need for, and value of, security, especially for children, and to endorse the claim that 'a happy family is but an earlier heaven'. It comes to affect our attitude to our occupation, which has to function not so much as a vehicle for the fulfilment of personal ambitions, whether these be associated with wealth, power or status, but as both a practical means to provide for the material requirements of life for ourselves and our families and the means through which we can constructively find happiness in making a positive contribution to our fellow men and women. It comes to affect our attitude to our environment, in which we are likely to see ourselves as stewards responsible for maintaining, and where possible improving, every aspect of our physical surroundings and circumstances over which we can have control or influence, and to our possessions, from which we can come to be free from the burden of more than is necessary and to regard unnecessary consumption as obscene. It comes to affect, too, our attitude to our leisure, which should come to be used constructively for the benefit of not only ourselves but our families and the wider community and the means through which we can make provision for the regular exercise, enquiry, reflection, meditation and relaxation necessary to sustain us on our journey, and to our effect on others, which we must try to ensure is both positive and beneficial.

Of course, only broad guidelines have been suggested, and these amount to little more than a general direction. Each of us must find our own way within this kind of framework (there are, after all, many paths to the top of a mountain) and in so doing will no doubt require, whether directly or indirectly (such as through books), the assistance of others with knowledge and experience. Nevertheless, enough has been said to suggest that it can provide us with a coherent foundation on which we can base our approach to every aspect of our lives, set us on a life-long journey on which we can work through the implications of the guiding principles and benefit from the deepening experience, the increasing clarity of vision and the growing capacity for making the most of opportunities for love and service, and to enable us to live with serenity and purpose amidst the great turmoil and stress of the twenty-first century.

Yet, in conclusion, it must be said that it is not just a philosophy for the present century, rather, as those that have trodden the path before know, it is eternally true that if we seek to know ourselves, live simply and love, serve and respect others, we can find, even in this vale of tears in which there is hardship, brutality, suffering and sorrow, wisdom, purpose, peace and joy. In brief, by affirming life we can live. The journey, which has been described in many different ways through various approaches to religion, philosophy and psychology, and which no doubt will be described with new depths of understanding, even entirely new modes of thought, as man progresses, is the way, not to mere survival, but to real, committed and abundant life.

'Happy the man, and happy he alone,
He who can call today his own,
He who, secure within, can say,
Tomorrow do thy worst, for I have lived today.
Be fair or foul or rain or shine,
The joys I have possessed, in spite of fate, are mine.
Not heaven itself upon the past has power,
But what has been, has been, and I have had my hour.'

John Dryden's translation of Horace

SUMMARY

1. Much as we would prefer to know all the answers, we have to accept that life is ultimately a mystery.

2. If we are to live in harmony with ourselves, with others and with our environment we have to embark on an intellectual and spiritual quest to find out who we are.

3. If we are to benefit fully from life we have to attend to all aspects of our well-being – physical, mental, social, emotional and spiritual.

4. Although we should value the past and plan for the future we should endeavour to always be mindful of the present. Every moment is precious.

5. If we accept that what we are is of greater importance than what we have, we can learn to enjoy the advantages of living simply and, in so doing, benefit too our environment.

6. Whatever our views about both religious institutions and their dogmas, we are wise to acknowledge the contributions of the great spiritual teachers and to recognise the value of stilling our minds in meditation.

7. If we are to enjoy the love and respect of others, we have to be prepared to extend the same to them whoever they are, irrespective of such as race, colour, creed, gender, age or sexual orientation. They, too, are distinctive centres of consciousness.

8. We have to accept that we are all products of our environment, of our cultural, religious, racial and family background and are all, without exception, flawed and prone to failures and weaknesses. We need, therefore, to forgive rather than stand in judgement of the errors and shortcomings of our fellows.

9. By recognising the futility of trying to live our lives in isolation, we recognise that our lives are given meaning through co-operation with, and service for, others.

10. In accepting that life is a gift – whether a gift of God or simply of genes passed from our parents – and that we did nothing to bring it into being, we can learn to accept the restrictions that life imposes on us and to value what we have.

11. In coming to a sense of oneness with the world we accept that all life is deserving of reverence.

12. In following this approach to living we understand that it is entirely consistent with a peaceful, politically stable, and environmentally sustainable world.

And finally:-

'if we seek to know ourselves, live simply and love, serve and respect others, we can find...... wisdom, purpose, peace and joy'.